iMAC

2020

USER GUIDE

For Beginners and Advanced Level
Users in Mastering the iMac 27-Inch
Model and the Newest Version of iMac
OS

By

George Wilson

TABLE OF CONTENTS

4

CHAPTER ONE

INTRODUCTION

GETTING ACQUAINTED WITH YOUR iMAC DEVICE

NATIVE FEATURES OF iMAC:

➤ **3.5 mm headphone:** Apple iPhone headphones with microphone for high-quality sound for multi-media purposes like watching movies, listening to your favorite music, or making calls.

➤ **SDXC card slot:** Transfer photos, videos, and data from your iMac and iMac using high-capacity SD cards.

➤ **USB 3 ports**: Connect an iPad, iPhone, iPod, digital camera, camcorder, external memory, or printer quickly and easily. The USB 3 and USB 2 devices are supported by iMac USB 3 ports.

➤ **Thunderbolt 3 and USB-C ports:** They connect Thunderbolt 3 to USB-C devices or monitors. An adapter may also be used to connect Thunderbolt 2 peripherals, a monitor, or a projector.

➢ **Gigabit Ethernet port or 10 Gigabit Ethernet port (RJ-45):** Connect a router or modem to connect to the Internet, or connect to another computer to share files without To transfer WLAN. The 27-inch iMac offers the flexibility to configure the 10 Gigabit Ethernet port for higher connection speeds.

➢ **Power cord:** Connect the power cord through the armhole, insert it into the power port (on the back of iMac device), then insert the cord into an electrical outlet.

➢ **Power button:** To wake up your machine, press the power button.
   o Choose Apple Menu> Shut Down to turn off the iMac
   o Apple Menu> Pause to suspend.

➢ **The Display Unit:** The 21.5-inch iMac has a 4K Retina display (depending on the model). Notwithstanding, the 27-inch iMac has a 5K retina display with unique True Tone. For a more natural viewing experience, True Tone technology automatically adjusts the color of your screen to match the light around you.

Enable or disable the True Tone in the system settings.

➢ **Microphones and Speakers:** 21.5-inch and 27-inch models have built-in stereo speakers and microphones. A microphone in the 27-inch iMac provides studio-quality recording for podcasts, voice memos, live music, and more.

CHAPTER TWO
LIVE WITH YOUR IMAC

THE KEY FEATURES OF YOUR IMAC

❖ **Built-in microphone:** With this feature, you can record sounds directly on your iMac using the supplied iChat app, or talk to your friends live over a broadband connection.

❖ **Camera indicator light:** This indicator light is activated when the iSight camera is being used.

❖ **Integrated iSight camera:** Video conference with friends and family over broadband with iChat, take photos with Photo Booth, or record videos with iMovie.

* **Load Slot SuperDrive:** This is designed to detect, read and write on CDs and DVDs with standard size.
* **SD card slot:** If you want to transfer photos, data, and videos to and from your iMac system, the SD card makes it easy.
* **Built-in stereo speakers:** this feature lets you listen to music, movies, games, and other media files.
* **Built-in Infrared (IR) Receiver:** Use an optional Apple remote (sold separately) with an infrared receiver to remotely control Front Row and Keynote on your iMac from up to 30 meters away.

PORTS IN YOUR iMAC

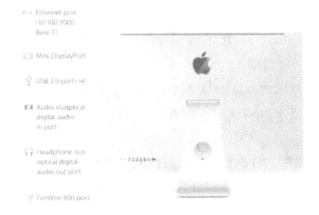

- ➤ **(10/100 / 1000Base-T) Ethernet port:** Connect or connect to a high-speed Ethernet (10/100 / 1000Base-T) network or a DSL or cable modem to another computer and transfer files.
- ➤ **Mini DisplayPort:** output connector compatible with DVI, VGA, and DVI.
- ➤ **2.0 USB ports:** You can connect iPod, iPhone, mouse, keyboard, printer, drive, digital camera, controller, and external USB modem.
- ➤ **Audio / Optical digital audio input:** Connect an external microphone or digital audio device.
- ➤ **Optical connector for digital audio/headphone output:** Connect headphones, external speakers, or digital audio devices.
- ➤ **FireWire 800 port:** Connect to external high-speed devices such as digital video cameras and storage devices.

OTHER ELEMENTS OF YOUR IMAC

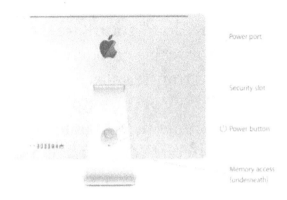

- **On/Off connector:** Connect the power cord to the iMac.
- **Security connector:** add a lock and cable to prevent theft.
- **Power button:** press to wake up or pause the iMac. Press and hold to restart iMac while troubleshooting.
- **Memory Access:** The iMac has at least 4 GB of memory installed as two 2 GB memory modules.
- **AirPort Extreme wireless technology:** Connect to a wireless network using built-in AirPort Extreme technology.
- **Bluetooth 2.1 + EDR wireless technology:** Connect wireless devices such as Apple Wireless Keyboard and

Apple Magic Mouse, Bluetooth cell phones, PDAs, and printers.

FEATURES OF WIRELESS KEYBOARD AND APPLE MAGIC MOUSE

Apple Magic Mouse

It includes the Apple Magic Mouse, Bluetooth wireless technology, laser tracking camera, and a seamless case that uses multi-touch technology to support multi-button, screen zoom, 360 ° pan, and iMac scroll control. Use mouse settings to adjust click, track, and scroll speeds, or add support for secondary buttons.

Apple wireless keyboard

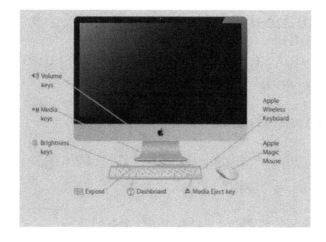

Combine wireless freedom with pre-programmed built-in function keys to work with your apps.

Multimedia eject key

Press and hold to eject a disc. You can also pull the hard drive.

Instrument panel button (F4)

Open the Control Panel to access your widgets.

Exposure buttons (F3)

Open Exposé to see all the open windows on your desktop at once.

Brightness buttons (F1, F2)

This increases or decreases the brightness of the screen.

Multimedia keys (F7, F8, F9)

Play, play, pause, or quickly forward a track, movie, or slideshow.

Volume keys (F10, F11, F12)

Mute, decrease, or increase the volume through the speakers or iMac headphone jack.

USING THE APPLE WIRELESS KEYBOARD

Your wireless keyboard contains two AA batteries that are compatible with your iMac. This pairing allows the keyboard and iMac to communicate with each other when they are wirelessly connected.

About the Indicator Light

The LED on the wireless keyboard serves as a battery indicator and status indicator. When you turn on the keyboard for the first time, the light will turn on for 5 seconds to indicate the batteries are good and then turn off. If you press the power button on the wireless keyboard and the indicator light does not come on, you may need to replace the batteries.

Connect the wireless keyboard to your iMac

If your wireless keyboard is not paired with your iMac, the indicator light will start flashing to show that your keyboard is in discoverable mode and ready to be paired with your iMac.

To pair your wireless keyboard:

A. Briefly press the power button to activate your wireless keyboard.
B. Choose Apple menu> System Preferences, then click Keyboard.
C. In the lower right corner, tap Install Bluetooth Keyboard.
D. Select the wireless keyboard and follow the instructions on the screen.

If you do not pair your keyboard with your iMac within 3 minutes, the indicator light and keyboard will turn off to save battery life. Press the power button to turn your keyboard back on so you can pair it with your iMac. The indicator light will glow for 3 seconds and then turn off when you have successfully paired your keyboard with your iMac.

Use your keyboard

Customize your keyboard using Keyboard Settings. You can change modifier keys, assign keyboard shortcuts to menu commands in Mac OS X or Finder, and much more.

To customize your keyboard:

1. Choose Apple menu> System Preferences.
2. Click Keyboard, and then click Keyboard or Keyboard Shortcut.

USING THE APPLE MAGIC MOUSE

The wireless Apple Magic Mouse that came with two AA batteries is now connected to the iMac.

About the indicator light

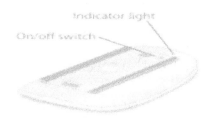

When the Apple Magic Mouse is on, the indicator light will illuminate for 5 seconds, indicating that the batteries are good. If you turn on the mouse and the indicator light does not come on, you may need to change the batteries.

Here's how to connect the Apple Magic Mouse to your iMac

When the Apple Magic Mouse is not paired with the iMac, the indicator light will start blinking to indicate that your mouse is in discovery mode and ready to be paired.

To pair with your mouse:

o Slide the power switch under your mouse to turn it on.
o Choose Apple menu> System Preferences and click the mouse.
o Touch Bluetooth Mouse Setup in the lower right corner.
o Select your wireless mouse and follow the instructions on the screen.

If you do not pair your mouse with your iMac within 3 minutes, the indicator light and mouse will turn off to save battery life. Turn the mouse back on by unplugging the power switch and plugging it into the iMac. After you have successfully paired your mouse with the iMac, the indicator light will be solid.

Use the Apple Magic Mouse

Use Mouse Settings to learn the Multi-Touch gestures you can use with the Apple Magic Mouse or change modes. Choose Apple menu> System Preferences, and click the mouse.

CHAPTER THREE

SET UP YOUR IMAC

Follow the steps below to set up your iMac. Don't turn on your iMac until you have completed step 4.

Step 1: Route the power cord through the hole in the handle as shown below, plug it into the power connector on the back of the iMac, and then plug it into an electrical outlet.

Step 2: Connect one end of the Ethernet cable to the iMac Ethernet port for Internet access or network. Connect the other end to a cable modem, DSL modem, or network.

Your iMac features AirPort Extreme wireless network technology.

To be able to use a telephone connection, you need an external USB modem. Connect the modem to a USB port on the iMac and use a phone cord to connect the modem to the phone jack.

Step 3: Switch the wireless keyboard and the mouse on

Press the power button on the right side of the Apple wireless keyboard and slide the switch under the Apple Magic Mouse to turn it on and use it with your iMac.

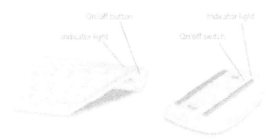

AA batteries are already installed in your wireless keyboard and mouse and paired with your iMac.

When you turn on the keyboard or mouse for the first time, the indicator light will glow steadily for 5 seconds to indicate that the batteries are good. The indicator light will continue to blink until the iMac is turned on and a connection is established. If your keyboard or mouse won't turn on, make sure the batteries are properly installed and charged.

Step 4: Press the power button on the back to turn on the iMac.

You will hear a noise when you turn on your iMac. Click the mouse to connect to the iMac.

If the keyboard and mouse are not paired, follow the on-screen instructions to pair them with your iMac. You may have to click the mouse once to connect.

Step 5: Use the setup wizard to configure your iMac.

The setup wizard starts the first time you turn on your iMac. The setup wizard allows you to enter email and Internet information and create an iMac user account.

If you already have a Mac, the Setup Assistant can help you transfer files, apps, and other information from your old Mac to your new iMac automatically.

If you don't want to protect or use your other Mac, the best thing to do is to turn off your iTunes Store purchases to play music, videos, or audiobooks.

If a computer is unauthorized, another person cannot play songs, videos, or audiobooks, and one more right to use is granted. For information about being rejected, see the iTunes Help menu under the iTunes Help menu.

If you are not using the setup wizard to transfer information at the first start, you can do so later using the migration wizard.

Step 6: customize your desktop and settings.

You can use System Preferences, your command center for most of the settings on your iMac, to make your desktop the way you want it. You can click the System Preferences icon in the Dock or select Apple> System Preferences from the menu bar.

Turn off the iMac or let it sleep

When you're done with your iMac, you can turn it on and off.

Put the iMac to sleep

If you're less than a few days away from your iMac, fall asleep. When the iMac is in sleep mode, its screen is blank. You can quickly wake up your iMac and skip the startup process.

The sleeping mode can be activated by following any of the steps below:

* ❖ Select Apple> Suspend in the menu bar.
* ❖ Press the power button (on / off) on the back of the iMac.
* ❖ Choose Apple menu> System Preferences, click Power Saver, and set the sleep timer.
* ❖ Press and hold the Play / Pause button on the optional Apple Remote for 3 seconds.

To wake your iMac from sleep mode, do one of the following:

* ➤ Press any key on the keyboard.
* ➤ Click the mouse.
* ➤ Press the power button (on / off) on the back of the iMac.
* ➤ Press any button on the optional Apple remote control.

When your iMac boots up, your PC apps, documents, and settings will be just as you left them.

Turn off the iMac

If you won't be using your iMac for more than a few days, turn it off. Choose Apple> Shut Down. Press the power button to turn the iMac back on.

Turn off your iMac before moving it. Moving your iMac while the hard drive is spinning can damage the hard drive and result in loss of data or an inability to boot from the hard drive.

CHAPTER FOUR

QUICK ACCESS TO FILES

Stacks automatically organize files on your desktop into groups so that you can easily find this important table. Right-click on the desktop and choose View> Use Batch.

USING STACKS

ARRANGING FILES IN STACKS ON MAC

You can use desktop stacks to organize files into groups. Every time you save a file to your desktop, it is automatically added to the appropriate batch to keep your desktop clean. The database contains several downloads for grouping files that you download from the Internet.

USE STACKS ON THE DESKTOP

You can group batches by type (such as images or PDF), date (such as Created or Last Opened), or Finder Tags.

You can do one of the following on your Mac:

✓ Click Batch to activate: click the desktop, then choose View> Use Batch or press Ctrl-

Command-0. You can also click Control on the desktop and then select Use Batch.

✓ Find files in the stack: swipe left or right on the stack with two fingers on the trackpad. Use your finger on Magic Mouse. You can also open the top file in a batch by double-clicking the file.

✓ Open a batch: click on the batch.

✓ Change the way batches are grouped: right-click on the desktop, choose View> Batch Grouping, and then choose an option such as Date Added. Control-click the desktop, choose Batch Grouping and then choose.

✓ Change the Batch View: Click the desktop, choose View> Show View Options, and change the options. Or, hold down the Control key, click the desktop, and then select Show view options.

Use stacks in the dock

The download stack in the Dock opens to show its contents in a grid. You can add files and folders to the Dock for quick access and even view them in bulk.

You can do one of the following on your Mac:

➢ Add files and folders: You can drag and drop a folder to the right of the section bar.

➤ Open or close a file or folder: click on. With the folder open, double-click an item to open it. Click Open in Finder to view a folder in Finder.
➤ Change the folder view: Click the control button, then choose how the items inside are organized, whether they appear as folders or stacks in the Dock, and how their contents appear (grid or fan).

MARKING FILES

To use the bookmark, select a file on your Mac, press the spacebar, then click the bookmark icon. With it, you can crop, sign, rotate, and draw images and PDFs right on your Mac desktop and even on your iPhone or iPad.

HOW TO MARK FILES

With markup on your Mac, you can write, sign, and draw crop or rotate PDF documents and images. If your iPhone or iPad is nearby, you can use Continuity Markup to mark the file on your device and view the changes right on your Mac, including using an Apple Pencil on your iPad.

- ❖ To use the continuity features, your devices must be Wi-Fi and Bluetooth enabled and meet the system requirements.
- ❖ Click the Bookmarks Tool while using Quick Look on your Mac. Or choose Highlight if you are using quick actions.
- ❖ It is also available in various applications such as Bookmarks, Email, Notes, TextEdit, and Photos. Use the tools to highlight an image or PDF document on your Mac. The tools available vary depending on the file type.
- ❖ If your iPhone or iPad is nearby, click the Annotation Tool to use the resume flag to highlight the file on your device. For information about using Apple Pencil on iPad, see Designing Markup Apps in the iPad User Guide.
- ❖ Swipe up from the bottom of your iPad to toggle between your brand name and the iPad home screen. To get back to your search, swipe up to reveal the iPad Dock, then tap the sidecar icon.
- ❖ Hold down the Option key while you drag an item to copy a shape, text, or signature. Use the yellow guides to align the elements.

If you don't like the changes and want to start over, click Reset.

Sketch: Draw a shape with only one path. If your design is considered the standard shape, this shape will replace it.

Draw: Draw a shape with a single line. Press your finger more firmly on the trackpad to draw a thicker, darker line. This tool is only visible on computers with a Force Touch trackpad.

Shapes: Click a shape and drag it to where you want it. With the blue handles, you can change the size of the shape. If it has green handles, use them to change shape. You can use the following tools to enlarge and reduce shapes:

Magnifying glass: Drag the magnifying glass to the area you want to enlarge. Slide the green handle to increase or decrease the magnification. Slide the blue handle to resize the magnifying glass. To enlarge an area further, you can use the yellow guidelines to create additional lenses and overlap them.

- **Magnify:** Drag the marker to the desired location. Change the size with the blue handles.
- **Highlight**: Enter your text and drag the text box to where you want it.
- **Sign:** If signatures are listed, click and drag them to the location you want. Change the size with the blue handles. To create a new signature, click the Signature Tool, click Create Signature if displayed, and then click the method that you want to create your signature for:
- **Use the Trackpad:** Click Trackpad, click the text when prompted, sign your name with your finger on the trackpad, and click Done.
- **Use your Mac's built-in camera:** click Camera, hold your signature (on white paper) in front of the camera so that your signature lines up with the blue bar in the window. When your signature appears, click Finish.
- **Use your iPhone or iPad:** Tap Select Device, then tap a device. Use your finger or Apple Pencil (on iPad) to sign your name on your device, and then click Finish.

- **Shape style:** change the thickness and type of the lines used, and add a shadow.
- **Outline Color:** Change the color of the lines used.
- **Fill Color:** Change the color used in any way.
- **Text style:** Change the font style or color.
- **Rotate Left or Right:** Click the left Rotate tool to rotate the object to the left. Keep clicking to keep rotating. To rotate the object to the right, hold down the Select key and right-click the Rotate tool until the object has finished rotating.
- **Crop:** Hides part of an element. Slide the corner handles until you can see the area you want to keep within the frame borders. Dragging the frame enable you to change the position. Click Crop when you're done.
- **Comment:** Use the markup sequence to comment on an element to draw or sketch with the nearby iPhone or iPad. The Annotation Tool will appear blue when your device is connected. Click the tool again to disconnect the device. Click Finish when you have finished marking.

If you are working in the Quick View or the Quick Actions window, your changes cannot be undone after you close the window.

ENLIST SIRI'S HELP

Click the Siri icon for tips on opening an app, finding a photo in your library, checking the weather forecast, converting currency, tracking game results, or completing the puzzle.

HOW TO USE SIRI

Use Siri on your Mac:

❖ Get quick answers and information, play music, and more to help you get on with everyday tasks.

❖ Siri can make suggestions about specific apps before requesting them.

TURNING SIRI ON

If you turned on your Mac when you first installed it, Siri might already be activated. If you wish to turn it on manually, take the following steps:

✓ On your Mac, choose Apple menu> System Preferences, then click Siri.

✓ Choose Activate. Ask Siri if it's not already selected, then click Activate.

When asked if you want to improve Siri and Dictation, do one of the following:

➢ Save Recordings: Click Save Recordings to allow Apple to save Siri voice and dictation interactions on this Mac. Apple can search for an example of the saved sound.
➢ If you don't want to share the recordings, click No Now.

Do one of the following:

o Use Hey Siri: Select the Hey Siri check box to use Siri, if Macs or AirPods support it.
o Set the keyboard shortcut: Tap the Keyboard Shortcuts drop-down menu and choose a different keyboard shortcut to query Siri or create your own.
o Choose how Siri communicates: click the Language pop-up menu and choose a language. Tap the Siri Voice pop-up menu, then choose the gender Siri speaks.
o Siri Mute - Click the Off button next to the voice response. The Siri response appears in the Siri window but is not spoken.

ASK SIRI

To ask Siri on your Mac, do one of the following:

- Tap on the Siri symbol in the menu bar.
- Say "Hey Siri" if your Mac supports it. Your laptop must be turned on to use Hey Siri. If Siri doesn't answer, open Siri Settings and make sure the "Hey Siri" hearing is turned on. You can use Hey Siri when your compatible Mac is locked or inactive.
- Say "Hello Siri" if connected AirPods or compatible headphones support it. If Siri doesn't respond, open Siri Settings and make sure the "Hey Siri" hearing is turned on on AirPods. You can also use Hey Siri while your Mac is locked.

When you use Siri, your device sends information from Apple, such as B. Your name and nickname, or the names and nicknames of your contacts, if you have set them up in Contacts. That way, Siri can better understand you and what you are saying. "What's My Name?" Prove it by asking. Alternatively, if you've added a work address, Siri can remind you to do things like go shopping when you leave work.

WAYS TO USE SIRI

You can use Siri to do a task for you, such as B. Get quick answers or turn on Do Not Disturb.

Use Siri Results

You can easily get Siri results from the Notification Center or use them in emails or documents.

You can do one of the following on your Mac:

❖ Open Result: To open it in Safari, just double-click a webpage or double-click a file or document to open it in the appropriate application on your Mac. You can also click a result to preview a Quick View window.

❖ Use or save a result: Drag and drop to add pictures or locations to an email, document, or desktop.

TURNING SIRI OFF

- On your Mac, choose Apple menu> System Preferences, then click Siri.
- Uncheck the Enable Ask Siri box.

STAY IN CONTROL

If your desktop is covered with open windows, let Mission Control automatically organize them on a level so you can see the window you want. To do this, just press the Ctrl and up arrow keys.

HOW DO I USE MISSION CONTROL?

Mission Control shows all the open windows on the Mac desktop in a single layer so you can find what you need. Full-screen or split-view apps and desktops that you create appear as thumbnails in the space bar at the top of the screen.

ENTER OR EXIT MISSION CONTROL

➤ From the trackpad: swipe up with three fingers to enter. Swipe down to exit. You can turn off or change trackpad movement according to the trackpad's settings.

➤ Entering or Exiting the Keyboard: Press the Control Mission button or use the Strip Control or press the Control-Up arrow keys to enter or exit the keyboard.

When you use a second screen and you go to Task Control on that screen, one screen only shows open windows and areas that you are working with.

SHOW OR MOVE ALL OPEN WINDOWS

• Show all open windows for the current application: Press the Ctrl-Down arrow keys. When Exposé is selected in the trackpad settings, you can swipe down with three fingers. Press the buttons again or slide your finger down to return to the desktop.

COPY OR MOVE OBJECTS WITH MISSION CONTROL

- Copy text or pictures between windows: after copying the item, type Task Control to display all open windows, click a window, and paste the item.
- Download / move a file or folder to the desktop: drag the item out of a window, press Command-Task Control to move all windows aside, and display the desktop. Then drop the item.

CHAPTER FIVE

HELPFUL APPLICATIONS FOR YOUR ACTIVITIES

GET YOUR BEST INFORMATION

The Photos app has powerful editing tools on your Mac that will help you edit photos like a pro, even if you are a beginner. You can fix red eyes, make colors more vivid, adjust lighting, and much more.

HOW TO EDIT PHOTOS

You can use photo editing tools to make simple changes like rotating or cropping your photos to get the best frame.

When you edit a photo, Photos retains the original, so you can always undo your changes and return to the original look.

Changes you make to a photo are reflected wherever they appear in your photo library - copies of every album, project, and so on.

Edit a Photo

In the Photos app on your Mac, you can do one of the following:

✓ Double-click a photo thumbnail, then click Edit on the toolbar.

✓ Select a photo thumbnail and press Back.

Do one of the following:

➢ **Customize Settings**: Click the Set button to display the configuration tools. See how to customize your lighting, photo pose, and more.

➢ **Apply filters:** click the filters to see the filters you can apply to change the look of your photo. See Use a filter to change the look of a photo.

➢ **Crop the picture:** Click Crop to view options for cropping a photo. See cropping and straightening photos.

➢ **Rotate Photo:** Click the Rotate button on the toolbar to rotate the image counterclockwise. Hold down the Option key while you click the button to rotate the image clockwise.

➢ **Auto-Enhance a Photo:** Click the Enhance button to automatically adjust the color and contrast of your photo. Press Command-Z or click Restore Original to undo your changes.

➢ Click Finish or Return to quit editing.

While editing a photo, you can press the arrow keys to switch to other photos.

COPY A PHOTO

Copy and edit the copy to create different versions of a photo.

- ❖ Select the photo that you want to copy to the Photos app on your Mac.
- ❖ Choose Image> Repeat 1 Photo (or press Command-D).

If you're copying a live photo, click Duplicate to include the video segment or Duplicate as Photo to add the still image only.

COMPARE PHOTOS BEFORE AND AFTER EDITING

When editing a photo, you can compare the modified version with the original.

- o In the Photos app on your Mac, double-click a photo to open it, then click Edit on the toolbar.
- o Click and hold the Do Not Adjust button or press and hold the M key to view the original photo.
- o Release the M button or button to view the photo with your changes.

COPY AND PASTE ADJUSTMENTS

After you've edited a photo, you can copy your adjustments and paste them into other photos. You can adjust one photo at a time.

You cannot copy and paste settings from the Touch Up Tool, Red Eye Tool, Snipping Tool, or third-party extensions.

a) In the Photos app on your Mac, double-click a photo you customized, then click Edit on the toolbar.
b) Choose Picture> Copy Settings.
c) Double-click the photo that you want to make adjustments to, then click Edit.
d) Choose Image> Insert Settings.

You can also click a photo and select Copy Settings or Paste Settings.

You can quickly remove changes in a photo. Choose Edit> Undo or press Command-Z to undo the last change you made. To discard all changes and start over, select the photo and choose View> Restore Original.

SORT MOVIES AND TV SHOWS

Dim the light, start and watch your favorite movies and TV shows right from your Mac with the Apple TV app - stream, buy or rent.

NAVIGATING AND VIEWING CONTENT

You can watch movies and TV shows in the Watch Now box in the Apple TV app.

Content search

- Open the Apple TV app on your Mac.
- Click Show Now.
- The next line shows the content that you added to Next, including the content that you viewed but not completed.
- Scroll down to view recommended movies and TV shows, including custom categories and private collections based on your viewing history.
- You can review an item's rating, description, available display options, and purchase or rental information by clicking the item.

PLAY A MOVIE OR A TV SHOW

When you find what you want to see in the Apple TV app on your Mac, click it and do one of the following:

- **Play an item:** Click Play. The play button can be used for free content, pre-purchased content, or content on Apple TV channels to which you have subscribed.
- **Apple TV + subscription:** Choose Apple TV + for free or sign up. You need to be guided by the on-screen directions to validate your subscription.
- **Subscribe to an Apple TV channel:** Free [Channel] Press Free and follow the on-screen instructions.
- **Buy or Rent a Film:** Click Buy or Rent, select the option you want and confirm the purchase or rental.
- **Buy an episode or season of a TV show:** Click Buy, choose the option you want and confirm your purchase.

SEE NEXT SCENES

In the Watch Now section of the Apple TV app on your Mac, scroll to the next line to see the shows you recently watched or added to the

Next list. To see more items, move the cursor to the beginning or end of the line, and then click the left or right arrow that appears.

Pictures and movies are displayed in the order you want to view them. For example, when a TV episode ends, the next episode will automatically appear in the next episode. If you have already watched a program, it will be displayed at the top of the "Next" bar when a new episode is published.

If you have an iPhone, iPad, iPod touch, or Apple TV and are connected to the Apple ID you use for Mac, viewing progress and chapter selection in the Apple TV app will stay in sync on those devices. For example, you can watch a program on your Mac and no longer watch it on your iPad, or vice versa.

UPLOAD A MOVIE OR TV SHOW TO UP NEXT
➢ In the Watch Now section of the Apple TV app on your Mac, click an item to view its rating, description, available viewing options, and purchase or rental information.
➢ Click on Add Next.

➢ The Add Next button changes in sequence to indicate that the item has been added.

REMOVE AN ITEM FROM UP NEXT

In the Watch Now section of the Apple TV app on your Mac, click Next. (If you don't see the Next button, click the item on the next line first.)

START WATCHING FROM THE NEXT EPISODE

- In the Watch Now section of the Apple TV app on your Mac, hover over an item on the next line and then click the Play button that appears.
- If the item cannot be played immediately, follow the instructions on the screen.
- Click the Close button to return to Show Now.

ENJOY THE LATEST SONGS

You may wish to enjoy listening to your favorite music with the Music app on your Mac while busy with activities. Subscribe to Apple Music and choose from millions of songs to stream, download, and play whenever you need fresh inspiration.

HOW CAN YOU JOIN APPLE MUSIC?

You can access millions of songs and music videos with Apple Music. If you're an Apple Music subscriber, here's what you can do:

➢ Play recommended songs on up to 10 computers and devices
➢ Download songs so you can hear them even when you are not connected to the Internet.
➢ See what Apple Music contributors are listening to and subscribe to playlists
➢ Apple Music Radio - Custom-made stations that you can listen to all day.
➢ Create an Apple Music profile and discover new music with your friends by sharing playlists and the music you are listening to.

SUBSCRIBE TO APPLE MUSIC

On your Mac,

❖ In the Music app, choose Account> Join Apple Music.
❖ Instructions are displayed on the screen. Follow these instructions.

Use your Apple ID to sign in if necessary. If you don't have an Apple ID, you can create an Apple ID in the configuration.

For the new Apple Music subscriber, the subscription is free for a trial period. At the end of the trial period, your subscription will be renewed every month.

Any music in the Music Library that isn't in Apple Music is automatically downloaded to iCloud so you can access your other computers and devices.

FIND YOUR NEXT FAVORITE APP

The App Store on Mac is a great way to discover new and updated apps, games, tips, tutorials, and even videos to test how an app works before you download it.

HOW TO RECEIVE APPLICATIONS

You can search for an app or search the App Store for the perfect app. You can purchase the app you want with your Apple ID or use a download code or gift card.

To change your download and purchase preferences, choose Apple menu> System Preferences> Apple ID, click Media & Purchases in the sidebar, and then choose your options.

FIND AND BUY APPS

In the App Store on your Mac, do one of the following:

- Search for an app: Enter one or more words in the search box in the upper left corner of the App Store window and press Enter.
- Check the App Store: click Search, Create, Work, Play, Develop, or Categories in the sidebar on the left.
- Click on a name or an app icon for a description and view customer reviews and ratings.
- To download the application, click the button with the price of the application or click "Download". Then click the button again (or use Touch ID) to install or purchase the app.
- An information bubble with the value of the application.
- You can pause or cancel it during the installation.

CHANGE THE DOWNLOAD AND PURCHASE SETTINGS

- ✓ In the App Store on your Mac, choose Apple menu> System Preferences.

✓ Click on Apple ID.
✓ Click Media & Purchases in the sidebar.
✓ Choose your options.

REDEEM APPLE MUSIC CARDS, ITUNES GIFT CARDS, OR A DOWNLOAD CODE

In the App Store on your Mac, click your name in the lower-left corner (or click Sign In if you haven't already), then click Redeem Gift Card. Enter the download code or password on your gift card.

If you have a gift card with a box around the code, you can use your Mac's built-in camera to redeem a gift card. Click Use Camera and hold the gift card 10 to 18 inches from the camera. Make sure the password field is in the center of the preview area and hold the card until it is used.

BUY SUBSCRIPTIONS AND CONTENT IN THE APP

Some apps sell additional content such as app updates, game content, and subscriptions. Enter your Apple ID (or use Touch ID) to make in-app purchases.

DOWNLOAD APPS BOUGHT BY OTHER FAMILY MEMBERS

If you're a member of a Family Sharing group, you can download eligible apps that other family members have purchased.

a) In the App Store on your Mac, click your name in the lower-left corner, or click Sign In if you haven't already.
b) Click the Recipients menu and select a family member.
c) To download an item, click the iCloud status icon next to it.

CHAPTER SIX

YOUR FAMILY –A PRIORITY

In the sidebar, common market and family sharing settings are selected, and on the right, the account and payment method for purchases are selected.

SHARE WITH FAMILY

With Family Sharing, your family can share their purchases (such as apps, music, movies, books, and TV shows), subscriptions, and storage, and get the latest information with a shared photo album, calendar, and reminders.

HOW DO I SET UP FAMILY SHARING?

Family Sharing allows up to six family members to share purchases from the iTunes Store, App Store, and Apple Books, an iCloud storage app, without sharing their accounts. Your family can also use Find Me on Mac, iCloud.com, iOS, and iPadOS to share a photo album and family calendar, and help find each other's devices.

Family Sharing Settings, which shows the sidebar of the various account options available to you, as well as the family settings for an existing account.

One adult handles Family Sharing and invites up to five people to join the Family Sharing group.

From the Apple menu, choose System Preferences, and do one of the following:

➤ If you're signed in with your Apple ID: Click Family Sharing.
➤ If you are not signed in with your Apple ID: Click Sign In. Enter your Apple ID information according to the instructions on the screen. Once connected, click the icon at the top of the System Preferences window, then click Family Sharing, which will now appear next to Apple ID Settings.
➤ Select Family in the sidebar.

To add yourself as a family organizer and add family members to the Family Sharing group, click the Add button and do one of the following:

➤ Add someone with an Apple ID: Enter the name or email address of the person you want to join the family with, click Next, and then follow the on-screen instructions.

➤ If the person you added is nearby, just enter your Apple ID and password. Alternatively, you can email that person to sign up.

➤ Create an Apple ID for a child under 13: Choose to Create an Apple ID for a Child Without an Account, click the Next button, and then follow the on-screen instructions.

Do one of the following to select the apps and services you want your family to share:

▪ Set up a common market: Select Common Market in the sidebar and set your options. Your family can share their purchases on the iTunes Store, App Store, and Apple Books so everyone can access them. The common payment method you choose will be used for all purchases. You can change the account used to make the purchase and opt out of giving your purchases to family members.

▪ Update iCloud Storage: Select iCloud Storage in the sidebar and click Update to update your iCloud storage plan from 200 GB to 2 TB. Family members can share the program with you or save their storage packages.

- Define location sharing: To learn how to set up location sharing on all of your devices, select Sidebar Sharing in the sidebar, then click More Info. You can set up location sharing so that all family members can see each other's location in Find Me and Messages. You can use Find Me on Mac, iCloud.com, and iOS and iPadOS devices.
- Screen Time: Select Screen Time in the sidebar, click Open Screen Time Settings, and select the options you want.
- Save Apple Music: Select Apple Music in the sidebar. If you don't subscribe to the Apple Music Family program, you can sign up for a 14-day free trial. When you subscribe to the Apple Music family, all family members automatically get unrestricted access to Apple Music.
- Subscribe to TV channels: Select TV channels in the sidebar. If you don't have a TV Channel Subscription, click More Info for information about TV Channel Subscription. When a family member subscribes, all family members

automatically get unrestricted access to TV channels.

- Subscribe to Apple News +: Select Apple News + in the sidebar. If you don't have an Apple News + subscription, click Learn more about Apple News + subscriptions. When a family member subscribes, all family members automatically get unrestricted access to Apple News +.
- Sign up for Apple Arcade (not available in all countries/regions): Select Apple Arcade in the sidebar. If you don't have an Apple Arcade subscription, click Learn more about Apple Arcade subscriptions. When a family member signs up, all family members automatically have full access to Apple Arcade.

Before purchases are available to all family members, each person must verify the Apple ID with which they share their iTunes Store, App Store, and Apple Books purchases.

KNOW WHERE EVERYONE IS

Whether it's teamwork, a friend's home, or dog walking, you can feel safe knowing where your children are. If your family uses the Find

My app, they can see each other's location on the map.

HOW CAN I SEE INDIVIDUALS' LOCATIONS?

When you follow a friend, you can view and tag their location, contact them using messaging, FaceTime, or email, and get location instructions.

Ask Siri. "Where's Solomon Actor?" Say something like that if the friend is already followed by you.

- In the Find Me app on your Mac, click People.
- Choose a name from your contact list.

If your friend's location can be found: They'll be shown on a map so you can see where they are.

If your friend is not found: "Location not found" appears under their name.

If you're not following your friend: "Can see your location" will appear under their name.

Click the Card Info button, and then do one of the following:

Label a friend's location: click Edit Location Name, choose an option (e.g. Home or Gym) or click Add Private Label, enter a name, then click Back. The tag will appear under your friend's name in place of the location.

Connect with a friend: Click Contact Us, then choose an option.

Click the instructions to navigate to a friend's location

Set up alerts: See Set location notifications for friends.

SET TIME LIMITS

Your Mac has screen time to make sure your kids have a safe and happy Mac experience. You can monitor and manage time spent on Mac and specific apps, and set time limits for apps.

HOW TO SET THE SCREEN TIME
You can do one of the following on your Mac:

- ➤ If you're using Family Sharing: Sign in to your Mac account and make sure you're signed in with your Apple ID.
- ➤ If you're not using Family Sharing: Sign in to your child's Mac account. From the Apple menu, choose System Preferences and click Screen Time. If you're using Family Sharing, click the drop-down menu in the sidebar, then choose a child. In the lower-left corner of the sidebar, click Options, then click Open.

Choose one of the following options:

- ❖ Include / Include Site Data: Select this option if you want the Screen Time reports to include details about specific sites they have visited. If you don't select this option, websites will only be listed as Safari users.
- ❖ Use Screen Time Password: Set this option to require a password to prevent Screen Time settings from changing and to allow additional time if limits are exceeded.

Optionally, do one of the following:

- ➤ Click Downtime in the sidebar, and then set a downtime schedule.

➢ Click Application Limits in the sidebar, and then set time limits for apps and websites.
➢ Click on Communication in the sidebar and define the dialog limits.
➢ Click Always Allow in the sidebar, and then select apps that are available at all times.
➢ Click Content and Privacy in the sidebar, then configure content and privacy restrictions.

PLAN FOR A QUIET TIME

When you need some peace, you can use Do Not Disturb to turn off distracting notifications from email, texts, or calls. Finally, the kids can do their homework or you can watch this movie non-stop.

HOW TO ENABLE DO NOT DISTURB

You can turn Do Not Disturb on when you need to focus on a specific task or pause notifications on your Mac.

ACTIVATE TEMPORARILY DO NOT DISTURB

You can do one of the following on your Mac:

+ Click the Notification Center icon in the menu bar, scroll down and then click Do Not Disturb.

✦ Hold down the Select key while clicking the Notification Center icon in the menu bar.

The icon is grayed out to indicate that Do Not Disturb is on. It stays until midnight or you close it or until you want to turn it off (as defined in the notification settings).

Schedule Do Not Disturb Program

- On your Mac, choose Apple menu> System Preferences, then click Notifications.
- Click Do Not Disturb in the sidebar at the top and configure the scheduling options.

You can set a time when you don't disturb you while your Mac is sleeping (useful when you sleep next to your Mac) or while you are viewing the screen (such as when giving a presentation).

CHAPTER SEVEN

SAFEGUARD YOUR DATA AND DEVICE

BACK YOUR FILES UP

Backing up your Mac is smart and easy. Open Time Machine and connect an external drive. Time Machine backs up everything automatically, so you can restore individual files or your entire system.

HOW TO BACK UP YOUR FILES

With Time Machine, you can back up your entire Mac, including system files, apps, music, photos, email, and documents. When Time Machine is on, it automatically backs up your Mac and files for hours, days, and weeks.

Time Machine keeps a copy of all data on your backup disk if you are using Time Machine on an Apple File System (APFS) computer. It also saves local snapshots of files that have changed on your internal hard drive so you can restore previous data.

Time Machine enables you to retrieve files that were accidentally erased or changed.

When you open Time Machine, you'll see a blurry screen with lots of Finder screens stacked to show backups. Click the arrows (or right-click the backup scheduler) to browse the backups and select which files to restore.

Time Machine takes local snapshots on computers using APFS. That notwithstanding, it is recommended that you back up files to other location besides the internal storage drive. You can use network drive, Time Capsule, or external hard drive to store your files. That way, if something happens to your internal drive or Mac, you can restore your entire system to another Mac.

Connect an external hard drive to your Mac and turn on the drive.

On your Mac, click Use as a backup disk and follow the instructions in Time Machine Preferences.

To open Time Machine Preferences, choose System Preferences from the Apple menu, then click Time Machine.

KEEP YOUR CODES SECURE

iCloud Keychain securely keeps your passwords and other data on Apple devices up to date. It remembers and supplements the information created in Safari.

USING THE iCLOUD KEYCHAIN

Your website credentials, credit card information, and Wi-Fi network are kept up to date via iCloud Keychain on all Macs, iOS devices, and iPadOS devices.

Account settings are also stored in iCloud Keychain, so your social media accounts can be automatically added to another Mac when you sign in with your Apple ID on that Mac.

Everything stored in iCloud Keychain is safe. protected against industry-standard encryption. iCloud Keychain can only be installed on another Mac, iOS, or iPadOS if approved.

SET UP iCLOUD KEYCHAIN ON YOUR MAC

- On your Mac, choose System Preferences from the Apple menu.
- Click on Apple ID

- Choose iCloud in the sidebar.
- Select Keychain and follow the instructions on the screen.
- Before you select Keychain, you need to configure iCloud.

APPROVE A DEVICE TO USE ICLOUD KEYCHAIN

If your Apple ID is configured for two-factor authentication, you can set up and approve another device to use your iCloud data. Simply enter the login password or the password of a device with iCloud Keychain installed.

If you're not using two-factor authentication and you've set it up to use iCloud Keychain on another device, you may be notified that the other device is trying to use your account. Follow these instructions to authenticate a device using iCloud Keychain.

You can do one of the following on your Mac:

- Click Next in the warning.
- On your Mac, choose System Preferences from the Apple menu.
- Tap Apple ID.
- Select iCloud in the sidebar.

➢ To the right of the keychain, click Options, then click Details.

➢ In the dialog box that appears, enter your Apple ID and password that you are using with iCloud, then click Allow.

CHANGE THE WAY NEW DEVICES ARE APPROVED

If your Apple ID is configured for two-factor authentication, when you set up iCloud on a new device, you can enter the login password and verification code from a trusted Mac or device so that the device can use your iCloud information.

However, you can change whether the iCloud Security Code can be used to approve the iCloud Keychain on new devices by clicking the Options button next to the Keychain in iCloud Settings. After using the iCloud Security Code, you can also change the iCloud Security Code or the phone number that you use to verify your identity.

➢ On your Mac, choose System Preferences from the Apple menu, click Apple ID, and then click iCloud in the sidebar.

➢ Make sure your keychain is turned on and your Mac is authorized.

- Click Options next to Keychain, and make changes in the dialog box that appears.
- iCloud Keychain Options Dialog box with fields to change the security code, the button to change the security code and confirmation number, and the option selected to confirm.

LOCK MAC WHEN IN IDLE STATE

If you need to get away from your Mac, you can help save the information by asking for a password to re-enable or exit the screen saver.

HOW TO LOCK THE SCREEN

To keep information off your Mac, you need to ask for a password when you wake up. When you return to your Mac, enter your username and password to continue working.

1. On your Mac, choose System Preferences from the Apple menu, click Security and Privacy, then click General.
2. Touch the desired password after the standby or screen saver has started.
3. Click the pop-up menu.
4. Select the time before a password is required.

The lock screen doesn't prevent other users from shutting down, restarting, and connecting to your Mac. If you think this could happen and you are using apps that won't automatically save your changes, you need to save your work beforehand. Exit your Mac.

You can use the administrator's name and password to unlock the screen for you or a typical user. However, you cannot do this for another manager.

FIND MAC FUNCTION

Find My Finder can help you find your Mac or other missing or misplaced devices even when you are not connected to the Internet

HOW TO FIND YOUR MAC

Find My is where you can find a lost device and play a sound to find it.

To find a lost device, you need to add it to Find My before it disappears.

VIEW THE LOCATION OF A DEVICE

❖ In the My Search application on your Mac, click Devices.

❖ Select the device you want to search for in the device list.

When the device is found: Appears on the map so you can see where it is.

If the device is not found: "Location not found" is displayed under the device name. If you want to be notified when the location becomes available, click the Map Info button and select Notify me when found. As soon as you find it, you will receive a notification.

PLAY SOUND ON A DEVICE

➢ In the My Search application on your Mac, click Devices.
➢ In the device list, select the device you want to play audio from, then click the Card Information button.
➢ Click Play Audio. With AirPods, you can left-click or right-click to find them one by one when they are separated.

IF THE DEVICE IS CONNECTED ONLINE: it delays for a while, then a gradually rising tone begins, and then it plays for about two minutes. The device can also vibrate.

IF THE DEVICE IS OFFLINE: With AirPods, when you open the Finder app, you will receive a notification on your devices the next time your AirPods are within range of one of your devices.

If your device is detected, you can turn it off by pressing any key before it stops automatically.

RECEIVE INSTRUCTIONS FOR A DEVICE

❖ In the My Search application on your Mac, click Devices.
❖ From the list of devices, select the device for which you want instructions, then click the Map Information button.
❖ Click Instructions.

The mapping application opens with directions from your current location to the current location of the device.

CHAPTER EIGHT

YOUR MAC –PART OF A LARGE TEAM

EXPAND THE MAC DESKTOP ONTO YOUR IPAD

Use your iPad as a second screen for your Mac so you can expand your workflow into a large work area and create things with Apple Pencil.

USE YOUR IPAD AS A SECOND SCREEN

With Sidecar, you can use the iPad in landscape mode as a second screen for your Mac. As with every other screen, you can enlarge your desktop by showing different apps or windows on your iPad, or by showing the same apps on your Mac instead.

A MacBook Pro next to the iPad Pro. The Mac desktop displays the main window of a photo editing application, and the iPad displays additional open windows of the application for advanced photo editing tasks.

The basket is a function of continuity. To use the continuity features, your devices must have Wi-Fi and Bluetooth enabled and meet the system requirements.

SETTING OPTIONS FOR SIDECAR

Ensure that your Apple login credentials for your Mac and iPad are the same.

On your Mac, choose Apple menu> System Preferences, then click Sidecar.

Configure the display options for the sidebar and touchpad, and use Apple Pencil on the iPad.

If you haven't signed in to your iPad already, click the Connect drop-down menu, then select your iPad.

You can also connect using the AirPlay menu in the menu bar or the AirPlay display the drop-down menu in display settings.

You don't have to connect the iPad to your Mac to use Sidecar.

USE THE CAR

If you haven't signed in to your iPad yet, click the Airplay menu on the Mac menu bar, then select your iPad.

The sidebar menu appears in the menu bar. You can change the way you work with the iPad at any time from the sidecar menu.

Do one of the following:

- Move windows from your Mac to iPad: Move a window to the edge of the screen until the cursor appears on your iPad.
- You can transfer windows from your iPad to your Mac: Drag a window to the edge of the screen until the cursor appears on your Mac. Alternatively, while using an application, choose Window> Move Window To Mac.
- Use the touchpad on the iPad: Touch any button on the touchpad with your finger or an Apple pen. The buttons available vary depending on the application or task.
- Use gestures on iPad: Use basic gestures such as tap, pan, pan, and zoom to enter and edit text.
- Switch between the Mac and iPad desktop on your iPad: swipe up from the bottom of your iPad to reveal the iPad home screen. Swipe up and down to reveal the iPad dock. Swipe up in the center of the screen and pause to view the iPad Home app. Swipe up

to return to the Mac desktop, then tap the sidecar icon.

When you're finished using your iPad, click the Disconnect icon at the bottom of the iPad sidebar.

TOGGLING TASKS BETWEEN DEVICES

Handoff allows you to start a task on one device and run it on another. For example, you can initiate a message on your iPhone and then send it from your Mac.

HOW TASKS ARE ASSIGNED BETWEEN DEVICES

Handoff allows you to start something on one device and then get it on another device without focusing on what you are doing.

To use Handoff, your devices must meet the requirements of the continuity system. You also need to have Wi-Fi, Bluetooth and Handoff enabled in System Preferences (on your Mac) and Settings (iOS and iPadOS devices). You must be signed in with the same Apple ID on all of your devices.

When sharing is enabled, you can use the universal clipboard to copy and paste text, pictures, photos, and videos between devices.

ENABLE OR DISABLE HANDOFF

• On your Mac: From the Apple menu, choose System Preferences, click General, and then choose Allow transfers between this Mac and your iCloud devices (in the Recent Items section).

• On iPad, iPhone, or iPod touch: Go to Settings> General> Transfer and tap to enable the transfer. Tap to close.

• On Apple Watch: Open the Monitor app on iPhone, go to My Watch> General, and tap to turn on Enable Streaming. Tap to close.

HANDOFF BETWEEN DEVICES

✓ From your Mac to an iOS or iPadOS device: The handoff icon for the app you are using on your Mac is displayed on your iPhone (under the app picker) or iPad or iPod touch (under the Dock). Tap to continue working on the app.

✓ From iOS or iPadOS or Apple Watch on your Mac: Handoff icon for the app you are using on your PC

Your iPhone, iPad, iPod touch, or Apple Watch will appear on the far left of your Mac (or at the top, depending on the dock's location). Click the icon to continue working on the application.

You can also press the Command key to quickly switch to the application with the submit icon.

UNLOCK YOUR MAC FROM YOUR WRIST

Automatically connect to your Mac while using Apple Watch. You don't need to enter a password.

HERE'S HOW TO UNLOCK YOUR MAC

While using Apple Watch, you can use it to unlock your Mac or approve app requests without entering a password.

The auto-unlock screen says in the middle of the screen that your Mac is unlocked with the Apple Watch.

Make sure that you are signed in with the same Apple ID on your Mac and Apple Watch, that two-factor authentication is enabled for your Apple ID, and that the Apple Watch is enabled and unlocked to use these features.

Enable automatic unlocking and confirm with Apple Watch

- ❖ On the Apple menu, click System Preferences.
- ❖ Then click on Security and Privacy.
- ❖ Click General and choose Use Apple Watch to Unlock Apps on Your Mac (available if you have WatchOS 6 on your Apple Watch).
- ❖ If you have WatchOS 3, 4, or 5 installed on your Apple Watch, choose "Let Apple Watch Unlock Your Mac". (You cannot approve request requests.)

Before making a selection, you may need to click the lock icon at the bottom of the control panel, then enter an administrator name and password.

UNLOCK YOUR MAC

Wake up your Mac to idle by pressing any key on the keyboard or turning on the screen of a portable device. The screen indicates that your Mac is unlocked.

APPROVAL OF APPLICATION REQUESTS

If an app requires authentication on your Mac (for example, to view passwords, unlock notes or settings, and confirm the app installation), your Apple Watch displays a confirmation prompt from your Mac.

On the Apple Watch, double-click the button on the side to confirm the job request.

If you're not sure if your Mac supports Auto Unlock and Verify with Apple Watch, choose Apple menu> About Mac, and then click System Report. Click on Network in the sidebar, click on WLAN and correct the option "Automatic unlocking - Supported".

If you're a different user administrator on your Mac, you can sign in to your user account and enable automatic unlocking or verification with your Apple Watch as long as your Apple ID uses two-factor authentication and is on your Apple Watch. WatchOS must be installed.

SHARE FILES WIRELESSLY BETWEEN DEVICES

AirDrop lets you share documents, photos, web pages, and more with anyone close to you who is connected to the same Wi-Fi network.

HOW TO SHARE FILES WITH AIRDROP

You can send documents, photos, map locations, and web pages wirelessly to a nearby Mac, iPhone, or iPad using AirDrop.

With AirDrop on your Mac, you can send items from Finder, the desktop, or apps like Safari or Maps.

➢ If you are sending items from the desktop or a Finder window, click the control that you want to send. Select "Share"> "AirDrop" from the context menu and then select the device to which you want to send the item.
➢ If you're sending items from the Finder, click AirDrop in the Finder's sidebar and drag the item onto the device you want to send it to.
➢ From an application: Click the Share button on the application toolbar, select

AirDrop, and then select the device you want to send the item to.

RECEIVE ARTICLES WITH AIRDROP

When someone sends you an article using AirDrop on their Mac, you can accept and save it.

In the AirDrop notification on your Mac, click the OK drop-down menu, and then choose an option.

Find the article in the Downloads folder or in the app where you saved the article.

HOW TO SET UP AIRDROP TO RECEIVE ITEMS FROM OTHERS

o Open a Finder window on your Mac by tapping the Finder icon in the Dock.
o Click AirDrop in the Finder sidebar.
o In the AirDrop window, click the Allow Search pop-up menu and choose an option.

AirDrop uses Bluetooth and Wi-Fi to transfer data between devices. Bluetooth and Wi-Fi are most likely enabled on your Mac. If you don't, you'll be prompted to open it when you try to submit an article.

CHAPTER NINE

INCREASE YOUR STORAGE

There are at least 4 gigabytes (GB) of dynamic random access memory (DRAM) with double data rate 3 (DDR3) than the two 2 GB memory modules that come with the iMac. You can replace or install 2 GB or 4 GB memory modules up to 16 GB. The following specifications stipulate the memory module requirement that must be met:

➤ SO-DIMM format
➤ 1066 MHz, PC3-8500, DDR3 compatible (also known as DDR3 1066)
➤ Buffered and not registered

It is recommended that you have an Apple-certified technician to set it up.

MEMORY SETUP

The iMac has four memory slots. The two have at least 2 GB of storage units. You can install additional memory in the empty slots or replace the memory in the filled slots with 2 GB or 4 GB memory modules for up to 16 GB of memory.

Always turn off your iMac and unplug the power cord before setting it up

Memory. Do not try to install memory while the iMac is connected.

TO INSTALL MEMORY:

1. Choose Apple menu> Shut Down to turn off your iMac.
2. Unplug all power cords and cables from your system.
3. Place a clean, soft cloth or towel on your desktop. Hold the sides of the iMac and position it so the screen is on the surface and the bottom is facing you.
4. Lift the stand and use a Phillips # 2 screwdriver to loosen the three captive screws on the storage access cover. Turn it counterclockwise.

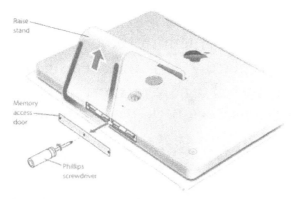

5 Remove the memory access door and set it aside

5. Remove the storage access cover and set it aside.
6. Open the tabs in the memory area.
7. To replace the memory modules, pull the tab to remove the installed memory modules. Remove the memory modules that you want to replace.

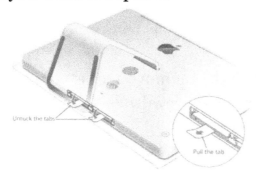

8. Install the new memory modules in the slots as shown in the slots on the right. If

you are installing additional memory modules, install them in the open slots. If you are replacing any installed memory modules, install a new memory module in each of the front slots that are closest to the display.

9. Press firmly and evenly into each memory module slot. You will hear a small click when the memory module is properly installed.

10.   Place the tabs in the memory area.

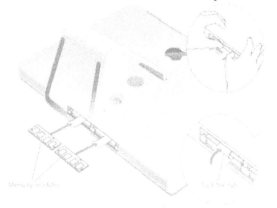

11. Replace the memory access cover and use a Phillips # 2 screwdriver to tighten the three retaining screws.

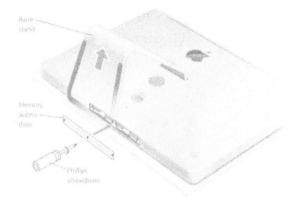

12. Hold the iMac by your side and stand it upright. The cables and power cord must then be reconnected.

13. Press the power button on the back to turn on the iMac.

Make sure to replace the storage access cover after installing the storage. The iMac will not work properly without a memory access port.

Make sure the iMac recognizes the new memory

After installing the memory, make sure that the computer recognizes the new memory.

To test the memory installed in your iMac:

✓ Start iMac.

✓ When the Mac OS desktop appears, choose
   Apple menu> About This Mac.

CHAPTER TEN

HOW TO FIND SOLUTION TO COMMON PROBLEMS IN iMAC

At times, you might have a problem with your iMac. When you have a problem with your iMac there is usually an easy and quick solution. If you have a problem, try writing down what you did before it happened. That way, you can identify possible causes of the problem and then find the answers you need. Points to consider:

❖ The application he was working on before the problem occurred. Problems unique to a specific application could mean that the application is not compatible with the version of Mac OS X installed on your computer.

❖ Any software that you recently installed.

❖ Any new hardware (such as additional memory or peripherals) that you have connected or installed.

COMMON CHALLENGING SITUATION IN IMAC

If the iMac is not responding or the pointer does not move

- Make sure the Apple Magic Mouse or Apple Wireless Keyboard is turned on and the batteries are charged. If you are using a USB keyboard or mouse, make sure they are connected. Unplug the sockets and plug them back in. Make sure they are safe.
- Try to force problematic apps to close. Hold down the Option + Command keys and press the Esc key. If a dialog box appears, select the app and click Force Quit. Then, save your work in any open applications and restart your iMac to make sure the problem is completely resolved.
- If you cannot force close the application, press and hold the power button on the back of the iMac for five seconds to turn off the computer. Unplug the power cord from the iMac. Then plug the power cord back in and press the power button to turn on the iMac.

IF YOUR IMAC FREEZES ON STARTUP OR DISPLAYS A BLINKING QUESTION MARK

➢ Wait a few seconds. If the iMac does not start after a delay, turn off the iMac by pressing and holding the power button for about 5 seconds until it turns off. Next, hold down the Option key and press the power button again to start the PC. Hold down the Option key until your iMac starts, then click the arrow below the icon for the startup disk you want to use.

➢ After iMac starts, open System Preferences and click Startup Disk. Choose a folder on your local Mac OS X.

➢ If the problem occurs frequently, you may need to reinstall the system software.

WHEN THE IMAC REFUSES TO START

✓ Make sure the power cord is plugged into the iMac and a working electrical outlet.

✓ Press the Power button and immediately hold down the Command, Option, P, and R buttons until you hear the second startup tone. This parameter resets the RAM (PRAM).

✓ If you recently installed memory and your iMac beeps every five seconds, make sure the memory is installed correctly and is compatible with your iMac. Verify that removing the installed memory will start your iMac.

✓ Wait at least 30 seconds after unplugging the power cord.

BATTERY REPLACEMENT

Apple Wireless Keyboard and Apple Magic Mouse, two AA batteries installed. You can replace them with rechargeable alkaline, lithium, or AA batteries.

Replace the batteries at the same time as changing them. Be careful not to mix old and new batteries or battery types. Do not open or puncture batteries, turn them upside down, or expose them to fire, high temperature, or water.

IF YOU WANT TO REPLACE THE BATTERIES IN THE WIRELESS KEYBOARD:

1. Press the power button to turn off the keyboard.
2. Remove the battery compartment cover with a coin.

3. Slide the two AA batteries into the battery compartment as shown below.

4. Replace the battery compartment cover.

Press the power button to check the battery status. If the indicator light does not come on, you may need to change the batteries. To check the battery level, choose Apple menu> System Preferences and click Keyboard.

HOW TO CHANGE THE BATTERIES OF THE APPLE MAGIC MOUSE:

1. Slide the power switch under your mouse to turn it off.
2. Pull the latch down to remove the battery cover.

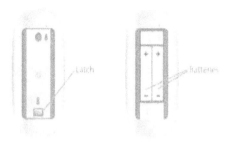

3. Insert the batteries with the positive ends facing up as shown above.
4. Change the cover and activate the mouse.

You may have to click once to reconnect the Apple Magic Mouse to your iMac.

To check the battery status, activate the mouse by dragging the on/off button. If the indicator light does not come on, you may need to change the batteries.

USING THE APPLE MATERIAL (HARDWARE) TEST

If you suspect that there is a problem with your iMac hardware, use the Apple Hardware Test application to determine if there is a problem with any of your computer components.

HOW TO USE THE APPLE HARDWARE TEST:

➤ If you are using it, disconnect any external devices from the iMac except the keyboard and USB mouse.
➤ Hold down D to restart iMac.
➤ When the Apple Hardware Test Language selection screen appears, select the language you want to use.
➤ Press Enter / Right-click.
➤ After approximately 45 seconds, the Apple Main Hardware Test screen will appear. The instructions will appear on the screen. Follow these instructions.
➤ If the Apple Hardware Test detects a problem, it will display an error code. Before you view the support options, write down the error code.

If this procedure doesn't work, you can insert the Applications Install DVD that came with your iMac to use Apple Hardware Test.

INTERNET CONNECTION PROBLEMS

The iMac has the Network Setup Assistant application to help you connect to the Internet. Open System Preferences and click Network.

Click the Help button to open the Network Setup Wizard.

HOW TO USE THE NETWORK DIAGNOSTICS:

- Choose Apple menu> System Preferences.
- Click Network, then click Help.
- Click Diagnostics to open the network diagnostics.
- Follow the instructions on the screen.

If Network Diagnostics doesn't fix the problem, there may be a problem with the Internet Service Provider (ISP) you are trying to connect to, an external device that you are connecting to the ISP, or the server that you are trying to connect to Want to connect. access.

INTERNET CONNECTIONS VIA CABLE MODEM, DSL AND LAN MODEM

Make sure that all modem cables are securely connected, including the modem cable, the modem cable to the computer, and the modem cable to the electrical outlet. Also, check the cables and power supplies of an Ethernet hub or router.

TURN THE MODEM OFF AND ON AGAIN AND RESET THE MODEM HARDWARE

Turn off the DSL cable or modem for a few minutes, then turn it on again. Some ISPs recommend disconnecting the power cord from the modem. If your modem has a reset button, you can press it before or after switching it off and on.

PPPoE CONNECTIONS

If you can't connect to your ISP using Point-to-Point Protocol over Ethernet (PPPoE), make sure you have entered the correct information in your network settings.

To enter the PPPoE configuration:

1. Choose Apple menu> System Preferences.
2. Click on Network.
3. In the list of network connection services, click Add (+) and choose PPPoE from the Interface pop-up menu.
4. Select an interface for the PPPoE service from the Ethernet drop-down menu. If you're connected to a wired network, choose Ethernet. If you're connected to a wireless network, choose AirPort.

5. Enter your ISP information such as account name, password, and PPPoE service name (if required by your ISP).
6. Click Apply to activate the settings.

NETWORK CONNECTIONS
Make sure the Ethernet cable is connected to your iMac and your network.

If two or more computers share an Internet connection, make sure that your network is set up properly. You need to know if your ISP provides a single IP address or multiple IP addresses for each computer.

If only one IP address is given, you must have a router that can share the connection. This is also known as NAT (Network Address Translation) or "IP Cloaking".

AIRPORT WIRELESS
COMMUNICATION PROBLEMS
If you have problems with AirPort wireless communication:

❖ Make sure the computer or network you want to connect to is working and has a wireless access point.

❖ Make sure that the software is configured correctly according to the instructions of the base station or access point.

❖ Make sure you are within range of the other computer or network access point. Having electronic devices or metal structures nearby can interfere with wireless communications and reduce this range. Moving or rotating the computer can improve signal reception.

❖ Check the AirPort status menu on the menu bar. Up to four lines of signal strength are displayed. If the signal strength is low, try changing your location.

KEEP YOUR SOFTWARE UP TO DATE

When you connect to the Internet, Software Update checks for updates for your computer. You can set your iMac to check for updates regularly, and then download and install updated software.

TO CHECK FOR UPDATED SOFTWARE:

1. Choose Apple menu> System Preferences.

2. Select the Software Update icon. The instructions will appear on the screen. Follow these instructions.

WHEN AN APP STOPS RESPONDING

In rare cases, an app can freeze. Mac OS X provides a way out of an unresponsive application without restarting your iMac. Exiting a frozen application may allow you to save your work in other open applications.

APPLICATION EMERGENCY CLOSURE:

1) Press Command-Option-Esc or choose Apple> Force Quit. The Force Quit Application dialog box appears with the application selected.
2) Click Force Quit.

The application will be closed and all other applications will remain open.

INSTALLING THE SOFTWARE WITH YOUR IMAC

Use the software installation discs that came with your iMac to reinstall Mac OS X and the applications that came with your computer.

You can choose "Archive and Load" to save your current files and settings, or "Erase and Load" to erase all of your data.

It is recommended that you back up your data on your hard drive before restoring the software. Since Clean & Install will erase your hard drive, you should back up your master files before installing Mac OS X and other applications.

MAC OS X SETUP

To install Mac OS X:

1) You need to back up your main files.
2) Insert the Mac OS X installation DVD that came with your computer.
3) Double-click Install Mac OS X.
4) Follow the instructions on the screen.
5) When you have completed the installation, you will need to restart your computer.
6) Follow the instructions in the setup wizard to configure your user account.

To reset your Mac OS X to its original factory settings, click Options in the Select Destinations area, then click Uninstall and Install. If you choose Uninstall and Install, a message will appear reminding you to use the

Application Installer DVD to reinstall the applications that came with your computer.

INSTALLATION OF APPLICATIONS

If you reinstall Mac OS X on your computer and choose Uninstall and Install, you will need to reinstall the applications that came with your computer.

When installing applications that came with your computer:

- Make sure you have a backup of your master files.
- Insert the application installation DVD that came with your computer.
- Double-click Install Bundled Software.
- Follow the instructions on the screen.
- When the installation is complete, click the Close button.

OTHER PROBLEMS

You can check and install the latest Apple software in the Software Update section in System Preferences. You can set your iMac to check daily or monthly. You can also check for updates manually. For more information, choose Help> Mac Help and search for "software update".

IF YOU HAVE DIFFICULTY INSERTING A DISC

- ❖ Slide the disc into the drive-in-one continuous motion until your fingers touch the tip of the iMac.
- ❖ Use only full-size discs.

IF YOU HAVE DIFFICULTY EJECTING A HARD DRIVE

- ❖ Quit all applications that are using the disc, then press the Media Eject key on your keyboard.
- ❖ Open a Finder window and click the export icon next to the tray icon in the sidebar or drag the tray icon from the desktop to the trash.
- ❖ Apple Menu> Sign Out of your user account by selecting "User" (your account name will appear in the menu) and then pressing the "Export Media" button on your keyboard.
- ❖ Hold down the mouse button to restart the iMac.

IF YOU HAVE PROBLEMS NAVIGATING WITH THE MOUSE

➤ If you have a trackball mouse and it is difficult to scroll, or the trackball does not rotate down or to the side, lay the mouse down and roll the ball while you clean it.

IF THE DATE AND TIME SETTINGS ARE REPEATEDLY LOST

• You may need to replace your internal backup battery.

FIND THE SERIAL NUMBER OF YOUR PRODUCT

Use one of the following methods to find the serial number of your iMac:

✓ Select Apple from the menu bar, then choose About This Mac. Click the version number with the words "Mac OS X" to toggle between the Mac OS X version number, build version, and serial number.
✓ Click the Finder icon and open / Applications / Utilities / System Profile. In the content pane, click Hardware.
✓ Look under the iMac stand.

CHAPTER ELEVEN

MACOS

macOS is the operating system that powers all Macs. You can use it to do things that you cannot do with other computers. This is because it is specifically designed for the material it is working on and vice versa. macOS offers a full suite of applications that are beautifully designed. It works with iCloud to keep photos, documents, and more up-to-date across all of your devices. It was carefully designed with security and privacy as priorities from the onset of the project.

Everything on the Mac works as you'd expect, from being simple and intuitive to use, to asking Siri to find a file and let your apps update automatically. Whatever you choose to use your Mac, there is less to learn and more to do.

Finder makes it easy to find, edit, and save files to iCloud Drive on your Mac. View files by icon, in a list, or by gallery view so you can quickly find a file by the view. Use the preview window to see the metadata of all of your files, quickly create ZIP files, and share them using the handy Share menu.

The dark mode gives a dramatic look to your desktop and apps that are focused on your content. Dynamic Desktop makes your Mac even more beautiful because delayed desktop images are always synchronized with the time of day. Stacks keep your desktop cluttered by automatically organizing files, images, documents, PDFs, and more into neat groups.

Spotlight makes it quick and easy to find what you want on your Mac, such as B. Documents, film times, and arrival and departure times. Type a few keystrokes into the Spotlight search box and Autofill will show you the results right away.

A simple two-finger finger on the right edge of your trackpad opens the Notification Center (the same one you use on your iPhone), which is where you can view any recently received notifications. You will also find the Today view here, which you can customize with useful widgets or helpful information from Siri searches.

Siri helps you get things done with just your voice. It also helps you do more. So, you can complete your document by asking Siri to let your partner know that you are away. And with Apple Music, Siri can be your DJ, recommending music the way you want and giving you more info on songs, albums, and artists.

PROCEED ON ALL OF YOUR DEVICES.

Your Mac works with other Apple devices in ways that no other computer can. When a call comes in on your iPhone, you can receive it on your Mac. And when your friends text you, you can reply from your Mac, iPad, or iPhone, no matter what phone they have. When you copy text or pictures from one device, you can paste them to another device using standard copy and paste commands. With Sidecar, you can use your iPad as a second Mac display to expand your workspace.

Privacy and security: Everything you do with your Mac is protected with powerful privacy and security features. Mac hardware and software are designed with advanced technologies working together to safely run applications, protect your data, and stay safe on the web. You can find a lost or stolen Mac offline or while you sleep with the new Find Me app.

Built-in apps: Apps are as powerful and stylish as your Mac. Every Mac comes with a collection of powerful apps. These are the same apps that you use on your iPhone or iPad to get used to in an instant. Everything works with iCloud, so your calendar, contacts, and notes are updated anytime, anywhere.

Media: Enjoy music, TV, and podcasts on three new Mac apps. Get all the important news from sources you trust in one place. Track your purchase and customize your watch list. View the top book titles from your desktop.

Creativity: Enjoy the best of photos and videos looking in a dynamic and stunning new look. Create professional music with a variety of sounds, instruments, amps, and a large collection of virtual drum and percussion instruments perfect for playing with your song.

Productivity: Create beautiful documents with surprising simplicity. Visualize your data precisely and convincingly in spreadsheets with images, text, and illustrations. Use powerful graphics tools and stunning movie effects to bring your ideas to life. And work with your friends and colleagues in real-time, whether in the city or around the world.

Contact: Easily manage all of your email accounts in one simple and powerful application that runs email services like iCloud, Gmail, Yahoo, AOL, and Microsoft Exchange. Send unlimited messages to any Apple device with the Messages app on your Mac and iPhone. FaceTime gives you unlimited high-quality video and audio calls from your Mac. Safely find a lost Mac with the new Find Me app on Mac, iPhone, and iPad

Internet: Surf the web seamlessly with an updated home page that gives you quick access to your favorite websites and frequent visits. Use Apple Pay to shop online in Safari with Touch ID on MacBook Pro and MacBook Air. Explore new destinations from your desktop with stunning 3D cityscapes like an overpass, point-to-point directions, and comprehensive directions.

iCLOUD ALL OF YOUR FILES ARE ON YOUR MAC.

All Apple apps use iCloud - that's the magic behind the seamless experience you have on all Apple devices. So you always have photos, videos, documents, emails, notes, contacts, calendars, and more on the device you use. And any file you save on iCloud Drive can be shared with your friends, relatives, and co-workers by sending a link. You can also use iCloud Drive to access files on your Mac from your iPhone or iPad. Everything is done automatically.

Accessibility: macOS comes standard with a variety of assistive technologies that people with disabilities can use to learn what the Mac has to offer and offer many features that cannot be found in other operating systems. With voice control, users can completely control their Mac, iPad, and iPhone with their voice. Features like VoiceOver, keyboard for accessibility, FaceTime, and text-to-speech also help you get the most out of your Mac.

DISCOVER ALL THE POSSIBILITIES OF MAC ACCESSIBILITY

macOS has powerful core technologies designed to power your Mac's most important functions. With Mac Catalyst, you can now enjoy your favorite iPad apps on your Mac. With SwiftUI, developers can find an easy way to build better apps with less code on all Apple platforms. By creating machine learning, developers can turn machine learning into applications faster and easier. With the support of virtual and augmented reality, developers can create exciting worlds to progress.

Compatibility: macOS makes it easy to transfer your files, photos, and other data from a Windows PC to your Mac. It also supports well recognized file types such as PDF, MP3, JPEG, as well as Microsoft Word, Excel, and PowerPoint documents.

CHAPTER TWELVE
TIPS FOR MACOS USERS
DESKTOP APPLICATION
MANAGEMENT

o **Enable Spotlight Search:** Use Command + Spacebar to open a handy search interface that you can use to find files on your Mac. Spotlight can do everything from finding files to answering basic questions to solving math problems.

o **Switching applications:** Press Command + Tab to switch between open applications. To switch between open apps, press and hold the Command key, then press the Tab key. Release when the application you want is highlighted.

o **Close applications from the toggle application:** In Command + Tab view, hold down the Q key and press Command to close an open application.

o **Hot Corners:** Well worth a visit if you are new to using Hot Corners. You can configure tasks to be performed when the mouse reaches a certain angle, such as B. Starting Mission Control, displaying the desktop, and much more. Set these as System Settings> Shipping Control> Hot Corners.

- o **Extended Hot Corners:** If you want to use Hot Corners but accidentally activate features, hold the Option key while installing Hot Corner. From there, Hot Corner will only activate if you hold down the Option key.
- o **Hide a Window:** To quickly hide a window on the desktop, just press Command + H. The application disappears in the background, but you can restore it by clicking the base icon or by using Command + Tab.
- o **Hide all windows:** You can press Option + Command + H to hide all windows except the application window you are using.
- o **Switch application windows:** If you have multiple open windows for an application such as Safari, you can use Command + Tilde (~) to switch between these open windows.
- o **Switching between multiple desktops:** If you have multiple desktops, you can quickly switch between them by

pressing the control key, then pressing the left or right arrow.

DOCUMENT MANAGEMENT

➢ **Open a folder quickly:** Hold down the Command key and press the down arrow key to open a folder in your Finder or on your desktop. To go back, hold down the Command key and press the up arrow key.

➢ **Clean up your desktop:** If you're on a cluttered desktop in macOS Mojave or later, right-click and choose Stacks for Your Mac to automatically organize everything by file type.

➢ **Delete files immediately:** To delete a file and skip the Trash, which saves files before deleting them on your Mac, select a file and press Command plus (+) Command plus Delete (+) keys at the same time.

➢ **Back up a file automatically:** If you want to create a duplicate file when you click on a specific file, just right-click and choose Get Info. then select the Fixed Pad field. Each time you open this file, a copy of it will open. This is ideal for templates and similar file types.

SAFARI

- **Safari window in the picture:** You can watch videos in Safari while doing other things. To do this, right-click a video twice to open a menu that offers a picture-to-picture function.
- **Safari picture-in-picture:** If the right-click method to open a video or watch YouTube doesn't work, there is another method. While playing a video, find the audio icon on the Safari toolbar, right-click it, and you should see the Picture to Picture option.
- **Copy links faster:** Press Command + L to highlight the URL bar, then press Command + C to copy the current URL into Safari. This method is faster than using a mouse.

FORCE TOUCH TRACKPAD

- ❖ Quick View: If you are using a Mac with the Force Touch trackpad, clicking and holding a link on a YouTube website or video will display a small preview of the content of the page you are on.
- ❖ Rename folders and files: If you tap a folder or file name, you can quickly rename

it. Click on a folder or file icon and you'll see a preview of the file.

APPLE WATCH AND MAC

➢ **Unlock with Apple Watch:** If you have an Apple Watch, you can use it to unlock your Mac. This is a very useful feature for those who don't know. To set it up, go to System Preferences> Security & Privacy, then switch to Unlock Mac with Apple Watch.

➢ **Apple Watch password authentication:** For macOS Catalina and Apple Watch users, Apple Watch can also be used as a password alternative so that you don't have to enter passwords as often.

MESSAGE CENTER

▪ Quick DND activation: If you hold the Option key and click the Notification Center icon in the upper right corner of your Mac's menu bar, you can turn on Do Not Disturb.

KEYBOARD'S ALTERNATE ROLE

➢ **Alternative mouse control:** You have the option of controlling the mouse pointer using the keyboard and activating it in input helpers. Open the Accessibility Settings and select the Alternate Control Methods tab in the Pointer Controls section. From there, turn on mouse activation and select the toggle to activate the mouse buttons when you hit the options button five times. The mouse buttons are then activated and the keyboard can be used to move the mouse.

➢ **Quick access to function button settings:** When you press any of the function buttons to activate broadcast controls, brightness, media playback, and more, hold the Select button as you press the button to access the appropriate setting options in the system settings for this key.

www.ingramcontent.com/pod-product-compliance
Lightning Source LLC
LaVergne TN
LVHW051703050326
832903LV00032B/3977